Illustrations by: Shiela Marie Alejandro
Visit her website:
https://www.bucketsofwhimsies.com

Summary: Stella and Roman visit Roger Williams Park Zoo in Providence, Rhode Island and interact with the zoo, staff, and animals for a fun and informative day.

ISBN-13: 978-0998800721
Printed in the U.S.A.

A healthy breakfast will grow your body and mind.
If you skip a meal, you will certainly fall behind.

Come join us on an adventure to the
Roger Williams Park Zoo.

We apply sun block to protect our skin.

How do you think animals protect their skin
from the sun's rays?

Diane Nahabedian met us at the welcome center and provided us with information about the park and animals.

She told us that the Zoo is home to endangered species and opened in 1872 making it the 3rd oldest zoo in the nation.

Meet our new friend Lou Perrotti.
He is helping the endangered New England cotton tail bunnies and timber rattle snakes.

His work ensures the future survival of these animals.

Roman was so excited to meet the timber rattle snake.

Lou Perrotti taught us that you pet a snake from the head to the tail.

Like a restaurant, the animals have their own kitchen and it's called a commissary.

The chefs for the Zoo prepare meals every day for over 160 animals including a komodo dragon.

The commissary serves fruits, vegetables, rodents, insects and other food to keep the animals healthy.

Do you know elephants may spend 12-18 hours a day feeding? The adult elephants can eat between 200-600 pounds of food a day.

The Alex and Ani Farmyard has Flemish giant rabbits, Guinea hogs, and a miniature donkey named Willy.

We fed a goat, collected eggs, and even milked a cow- REALLY!

The Zoo has three elephants named Alice, Kate, and Ginny.

Roman gave Alice treats when she was in the shower. Do you know that elephants eat grass, herbs, and flowers?

The Zoo had an elephant booth to teach us about their diet and teeth.

Do you know that an older elephant's single molar can be 10-12 inches long and weigh more than 8 pounds?

With monkeys, snakes, birds, and fish, the Zoo has brought the rainforest to Rhode Island!

Do you know that monkeys can be seen sitting or sleeping in pairs with their tails intertwined?

It's lunch time at the café!

PB&J, milk and an apple will give us nutrition and energy for the afternoon.

The giraffe is the tallest land animal on earth. Do you know a giraffe's neck is too short to reach the ground?

A baby giraffe is called a calf and will stand and walk within an hour after birth.

With long eyelashes, a third eyelid, and hairy ears, camels are specialized for desert living.

Do you know the hump we are sitting on stores fat and allows camels to survive for weeks without water or food?

Since 1782, the American bald eagle has been the symbol of the United States.

Do you know bald eagles are not bald? The word "balde" originally meant white.

Andrea Stein is the dean of education and teacher development at the Zoo.

Do you know that a ferret's favorite activity is stealing and hiding almost anything?

We met Jen Rudolph and the ambassador animals who spring up throughout the park to say hello.

The shoe covers are important to keep the animal's house clean of germs and bacteria.

All aboard the Carousel Express for a ride through the park.

Roman wants to be the conductor so I have to be the caboose.

We had so much fun and thank you for reading along.

Until we meet again-So long.

The End!

~Roger Williams Park Zoo and Carousel Village~

Located amid 40 acres of beautiful woodlands, the Roger Williams Park Zoo in Providence, Rhode Island provides visitors the opportunity to see animals from all over the globe. Naturalistic surroundings are home to more than 100 species of animals including a Komodo dragon, as well as zebra's, red pandas, African elephants, Masai giraffes, snow leopards, bears, anteaters, flamingoes, sloths, alligators, and more! Kids from two to 102 have the opportunity to feed giraffes and harbor seals, as well as an array of farmyard animals. In the summer of 2018, the Zoo will open its exciting new Amazon Rainforest exhibit complete with the flora and fauna of the region. At the core of the Zoo's mission is conservation and environmental stewardship for which the organization is the recipient of numerous awards for work done both locally and internationally.

Roger Williams Park Zoo is an accredited member of the Association of Zoos and Aquariums (AZA), and is home to many endangered species. As a result, the Zoo participates in cooperative conservation and breeding programs to help ensure the future survival of many endangered species.

Location and Contact	Daily General Admission
1000 Elmwood Avenue, Providence, RI 02907	Adults............................ …....$17.95
(401) 785-3510	Children (ages 2-12)...... …....$12.95
http://www.rwpzoo.org	Seniors (ages 62+)........ …......$15.95
visitorservices@rwpzoo.org	Toddlers one & younger...... FREE
Group Sales: (401) 785-3510 ext. 496	Zoo Members........................ FREE

~Membership~

Individual membership benefits for one adult.

- o 1 Year-$55.00

Family members benefits for 2 adults in same household and up to 4 dependent children under age 18.

- o 1 Year-$109

Grandparent's benefits for 2 adults in same household and up to 4 dependent grandchildren under age 18.

- o 1 Year-$109

Family Plus: All the benefits of a Family level, plus one free guest each visit.

- o 1 Year-$209

Zookeeper: All the benefits of a Family level, plus 2 free guests each visit.

- o 1 Year-$159

Patron's Circle, All the benefits of a Family level, plus 4 free guests each visit, recognition in our Gratitude Report, and invitations to select opening receptions and events.

- o 1 Year-$250

Meet the Educators

School & Education

Nature Swap

Community Groups

95449002R10015

Made in the USA
Columbia, SC
18 May 2018